When I attended the University of the Arts, an assignment for Jazz Theory class was to compose a jazz composition using any of the standard forms of 12, 16, or 32 bars, but the melody had to consist primarily of triads and some passing tones. At the time, it was common, like with many college students, to put just enough effort into their assignments to either pass the assignment or to please the teacher. I didn't want to do that, in fact many of my assignments I would always put my own spin on the assignment. And when the jazz theory professor gave the instructions, I immediately knew as to how the song would sound, which it would be similar to how Eric Dolphy improvised. I composed In Walked Dolphy in the spring of 1999.

Enjoy.

Andrew Hanna - January 2021

In Walked Dolphy

(C) 2021

Bb7
Ab7
Eb7
E7 Eb7 Bb7
9
A. Sax.
Pno.
Bass
Dr.
Solo Section
B
Eb7
4/4 Feel
13
A. Sax.
Pno.
Bass
B
Dr.

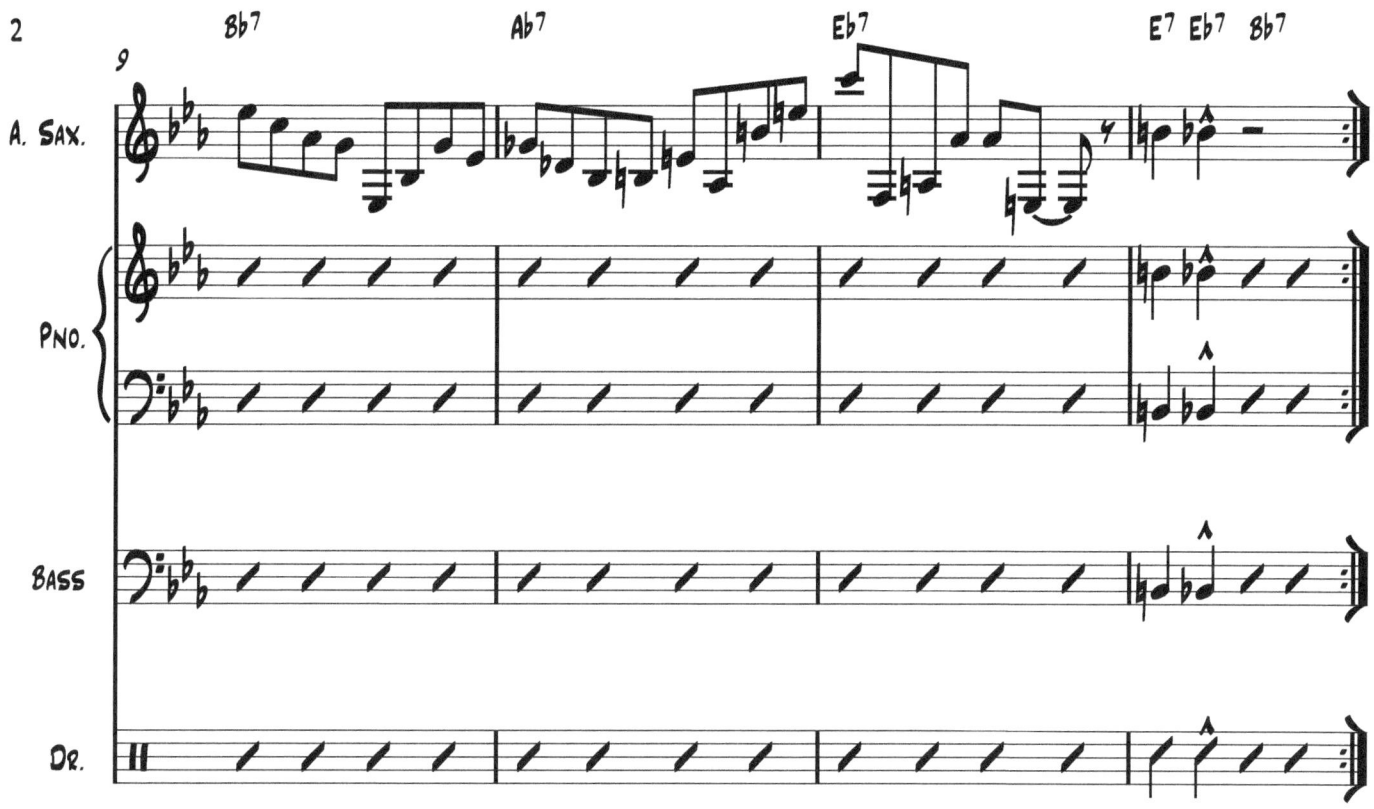

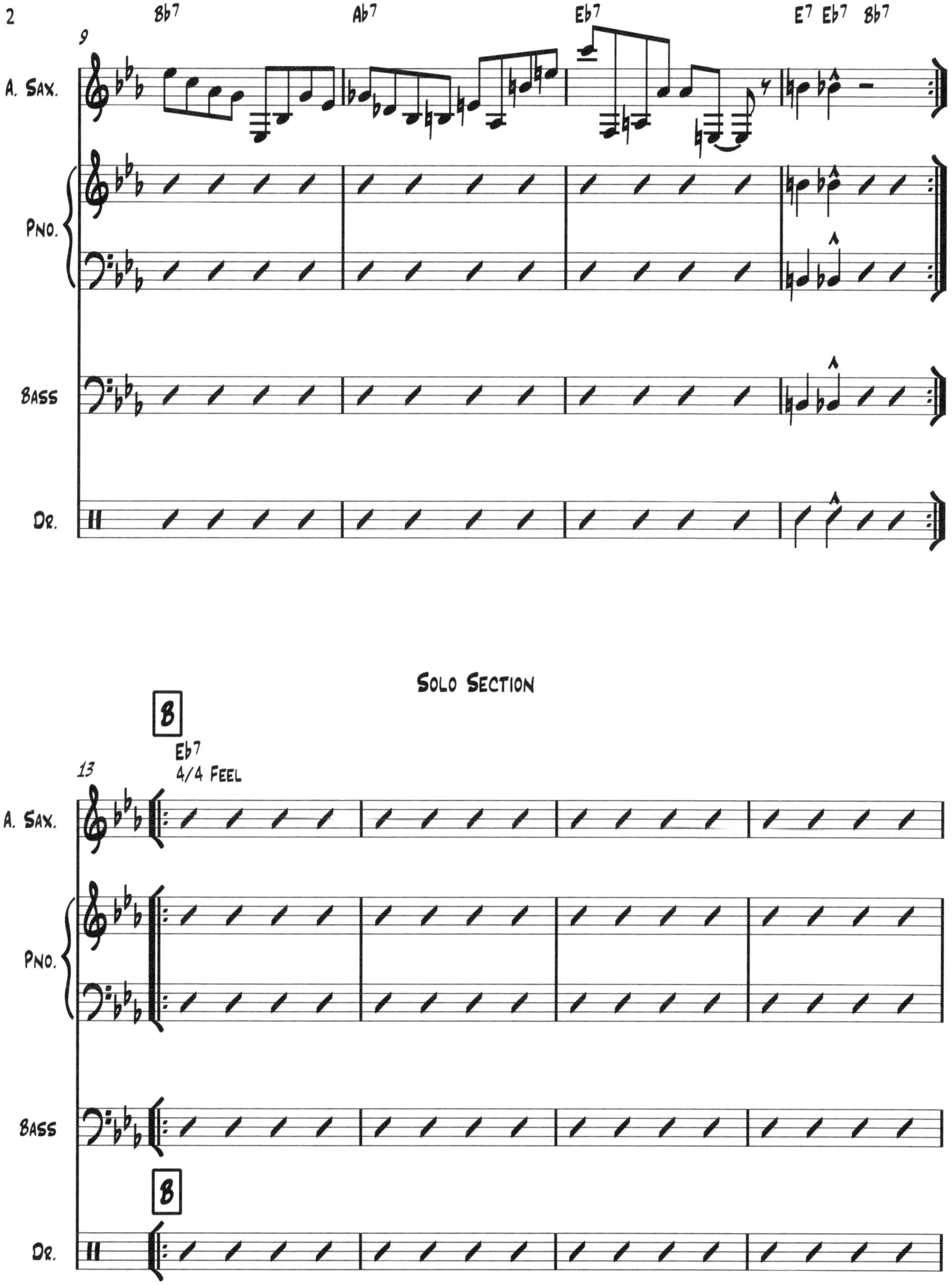

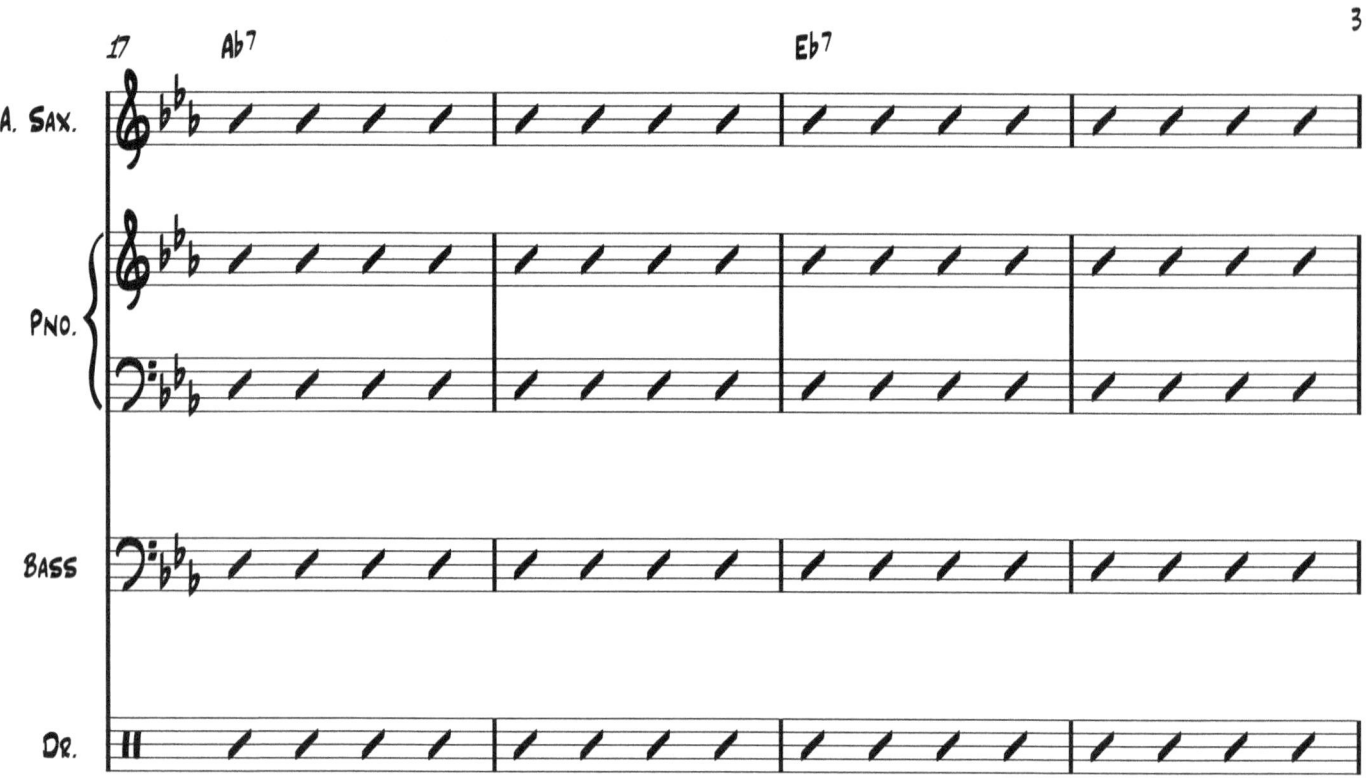
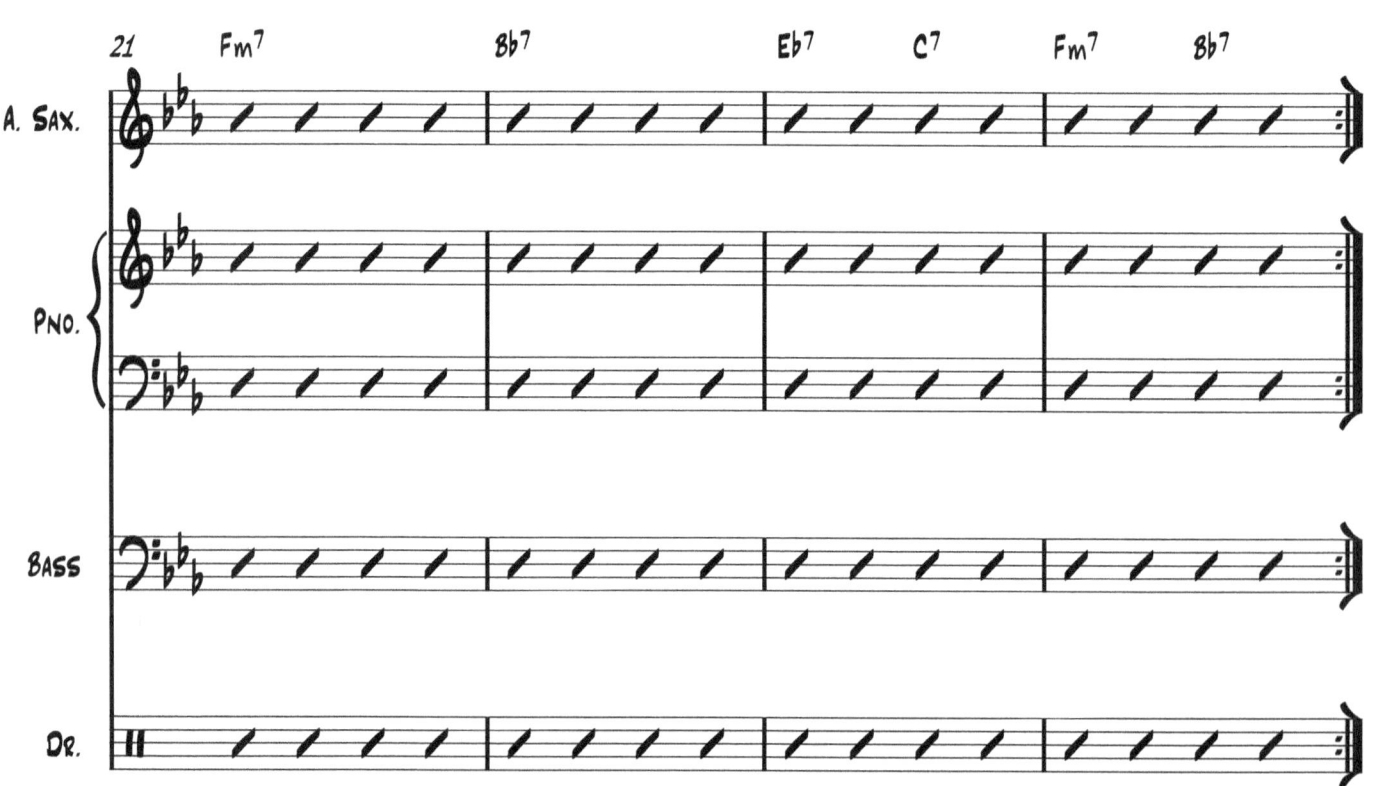

In Walked Dolphy

Alto Sax

Andrew Hanna

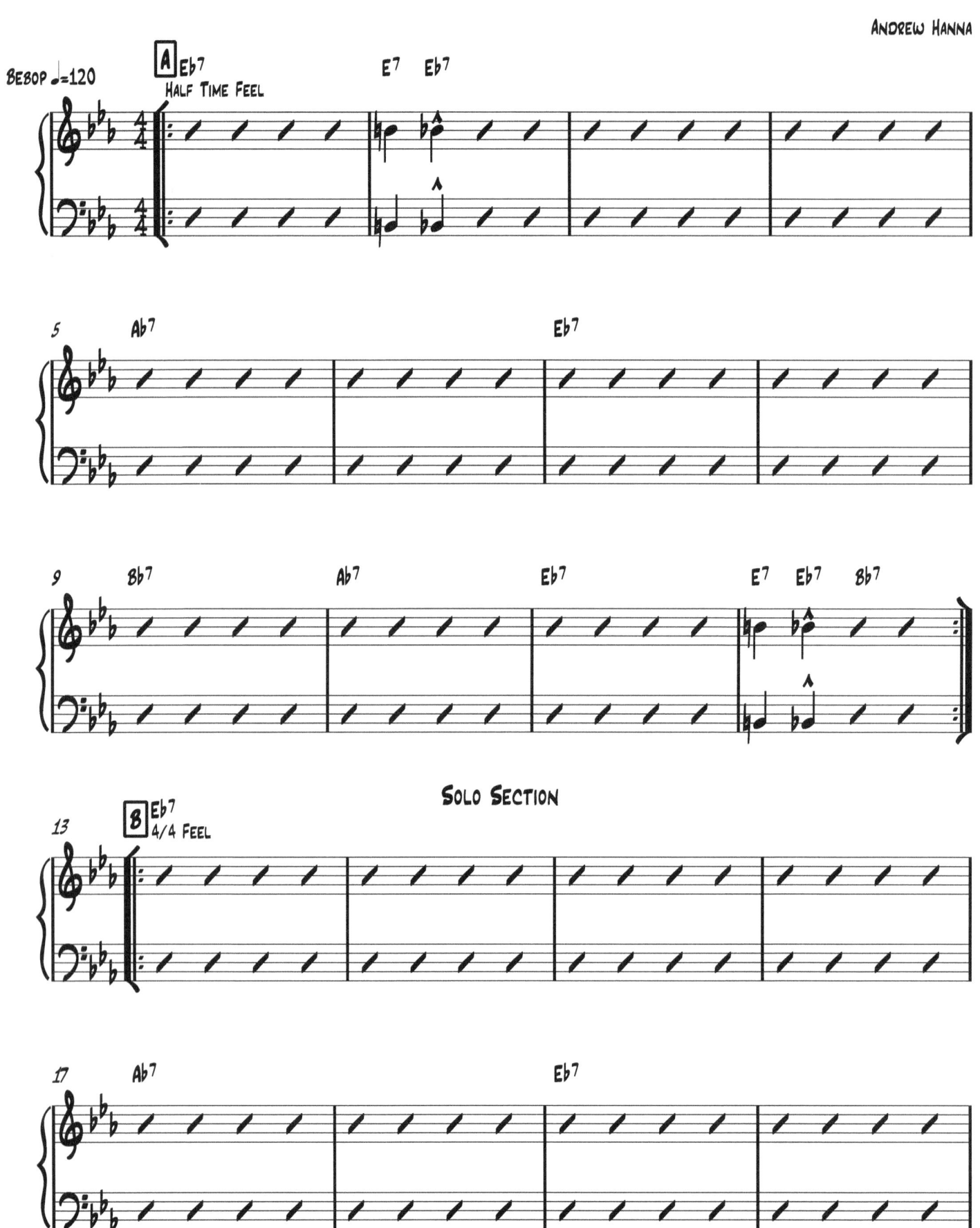

In Walked Dolphy

Bass

Andrew Hanna

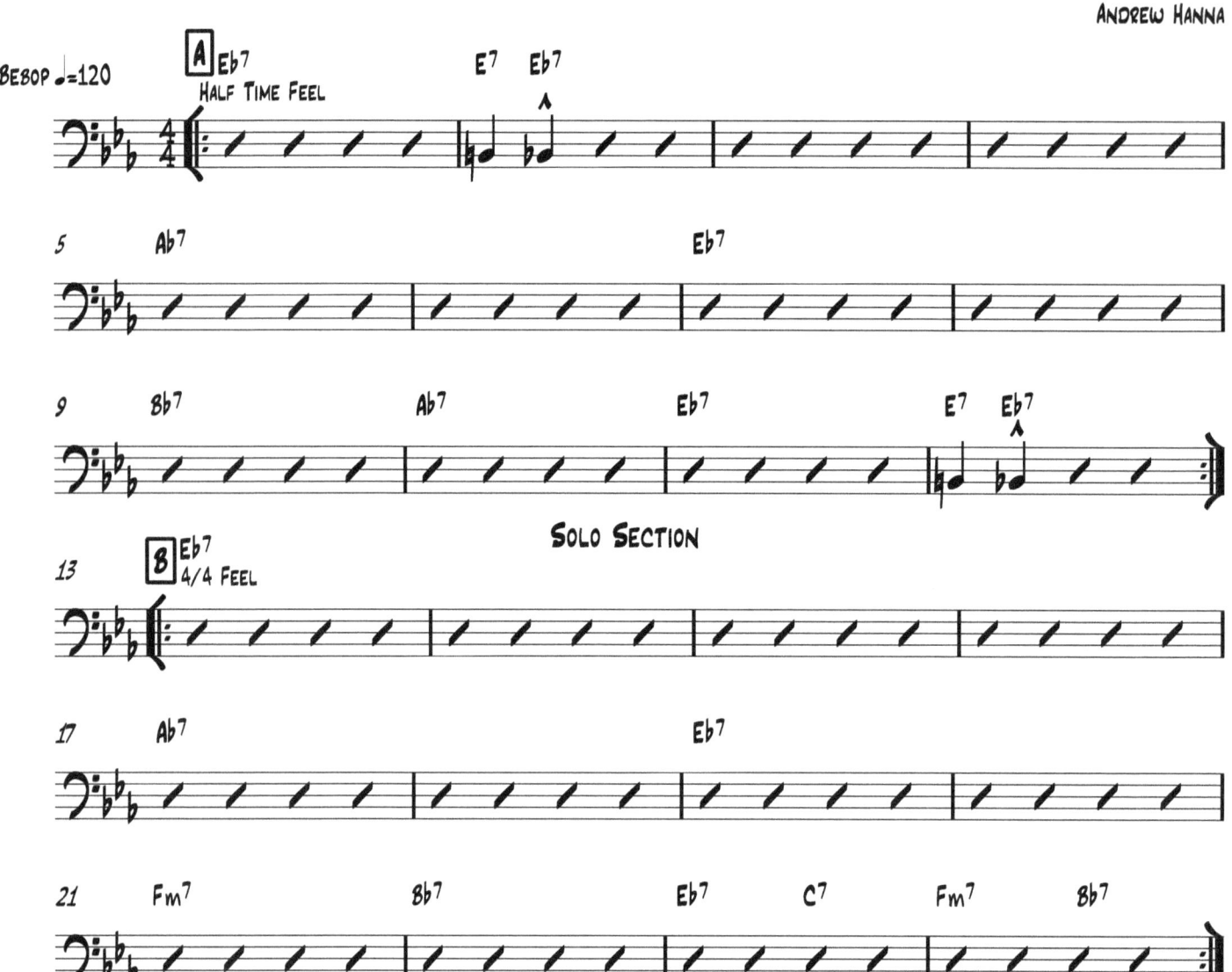

In Walked Dolphy

Drum Set

Andrew Hanna

Bebop ♩=120

A Half Time Feel

B 4/4 Feel — Solo Section

(C) 2021

C Instruments

In Walked Dolphy

Andrew Hanna

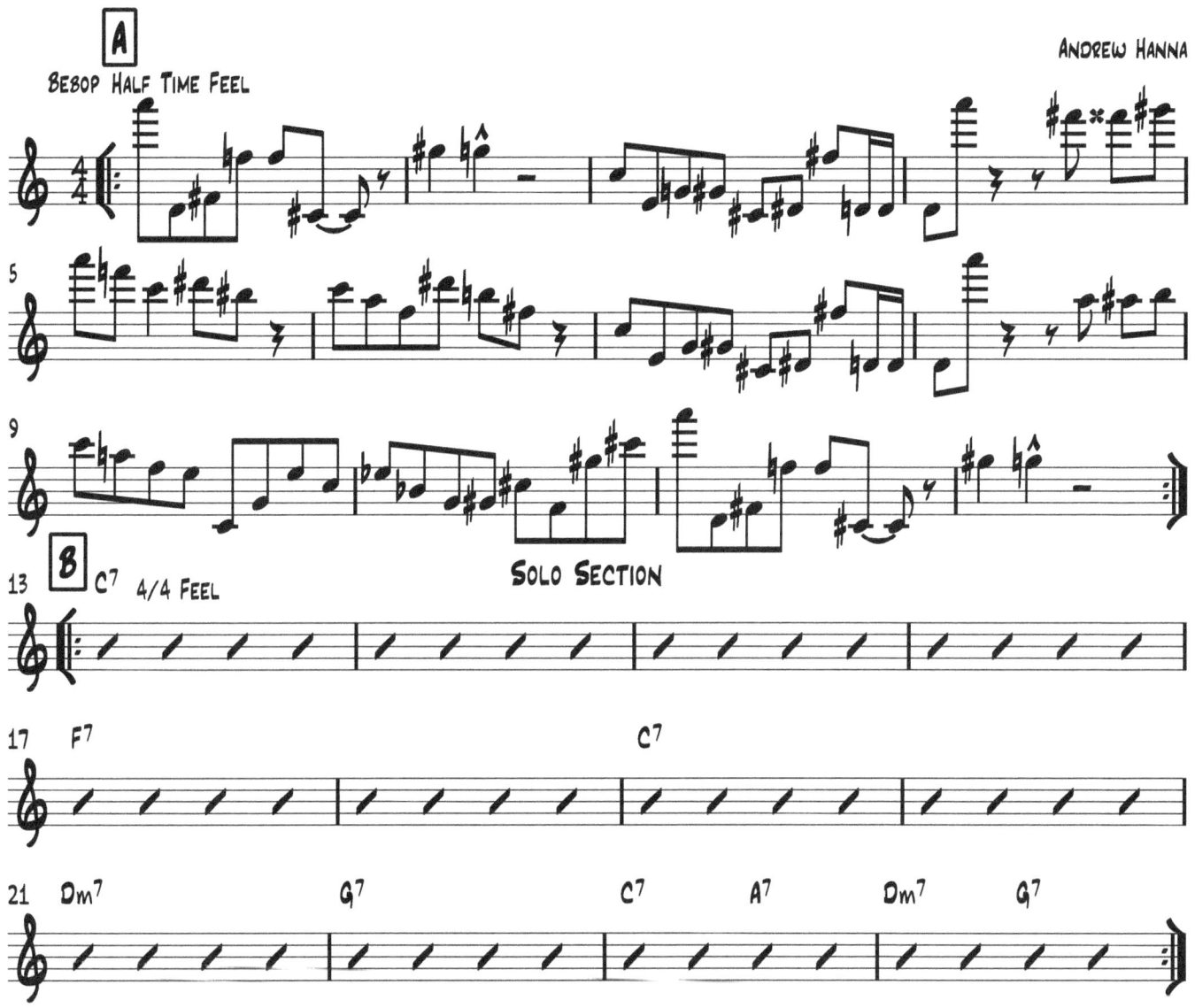

Bass Instruments

In Walked Dolphy

Andrew Hanna

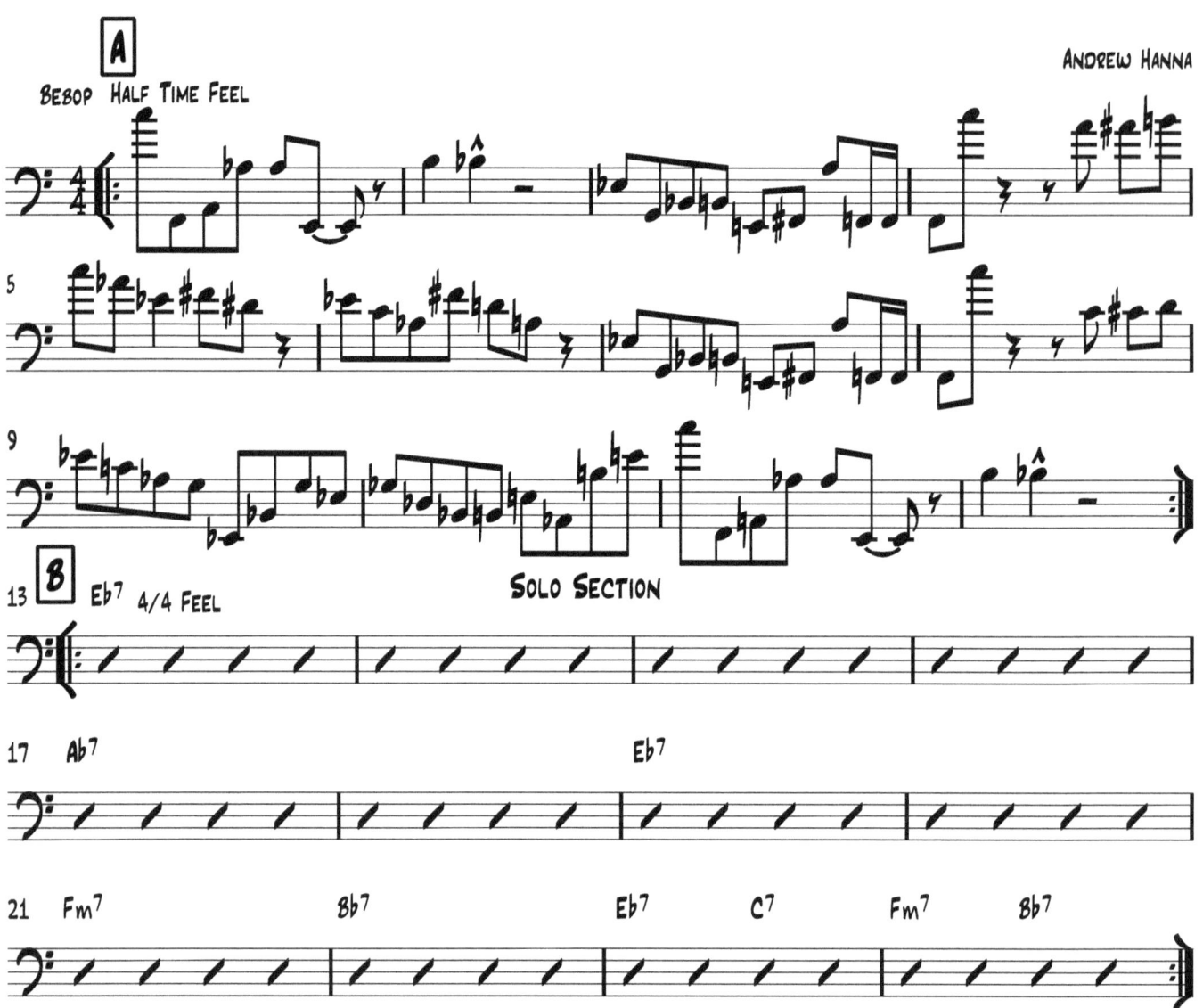

www.ingramcontent.com/pod-product-compliance
Lightning Source LLC
Chambersburg PA
CBHW082041080526
44578CB00009B/800